MEMORIES

COLECCIÓN CLÁSICOS CUBANOS # 26

Previous page, the entrance to the Bay of Havana, as seen from Casablanca.

EDICIONES UNIVERSAL, Miami, Florida, 2022

To Olga, my wife,
and to all the children and
grandchildren of families with
roots in Cuba, who were born in
liberty after their parents
and grandparents went into exile when
Marxism took over in Cuba.

Cuba from space. Photo courtesy of NASA.

Memories

BEATIFUL CUBA IN LIVING COLOR

RAÚL EDUARDO CHAO

...EDICIONES UNIVERSAL

Copyright © 2022 by Raúl Eduardo Chao

―――

First Edition, 2022
EDICIONES UNIVERSAL
P.O. Box 450353 (Shenandoah Station)
Miami, FL 33245-0353. USA
(Since 1965)
e-mail: ediciones@ediciones.com
http://www.ediciones.com

Library of Congress Catalog No.: 2022947550

ISBN: 978-1-59388-333-1

COVERS DESIGN: Luis García Fresquet.

FRONT COVER: **Morro Castle** at the entrance of Havana Bay and the most iconic view in Cuba, the **Viñales Valley**.

BACK COVER: a night view of the
Cienfuegos Tennis and Yacht Club in Punta Gorda.

All rights
are reserved. no part of
this book may be reproduced or transmitted
in any form or by any electronic or mechanical means,
including photocopiers, tape recorders or computerized systems,
without the written permission of the author, except in the case of
brief quotes incorporated in critical articles or in
journals. For information go to
EDICIONES UNIVERSAL

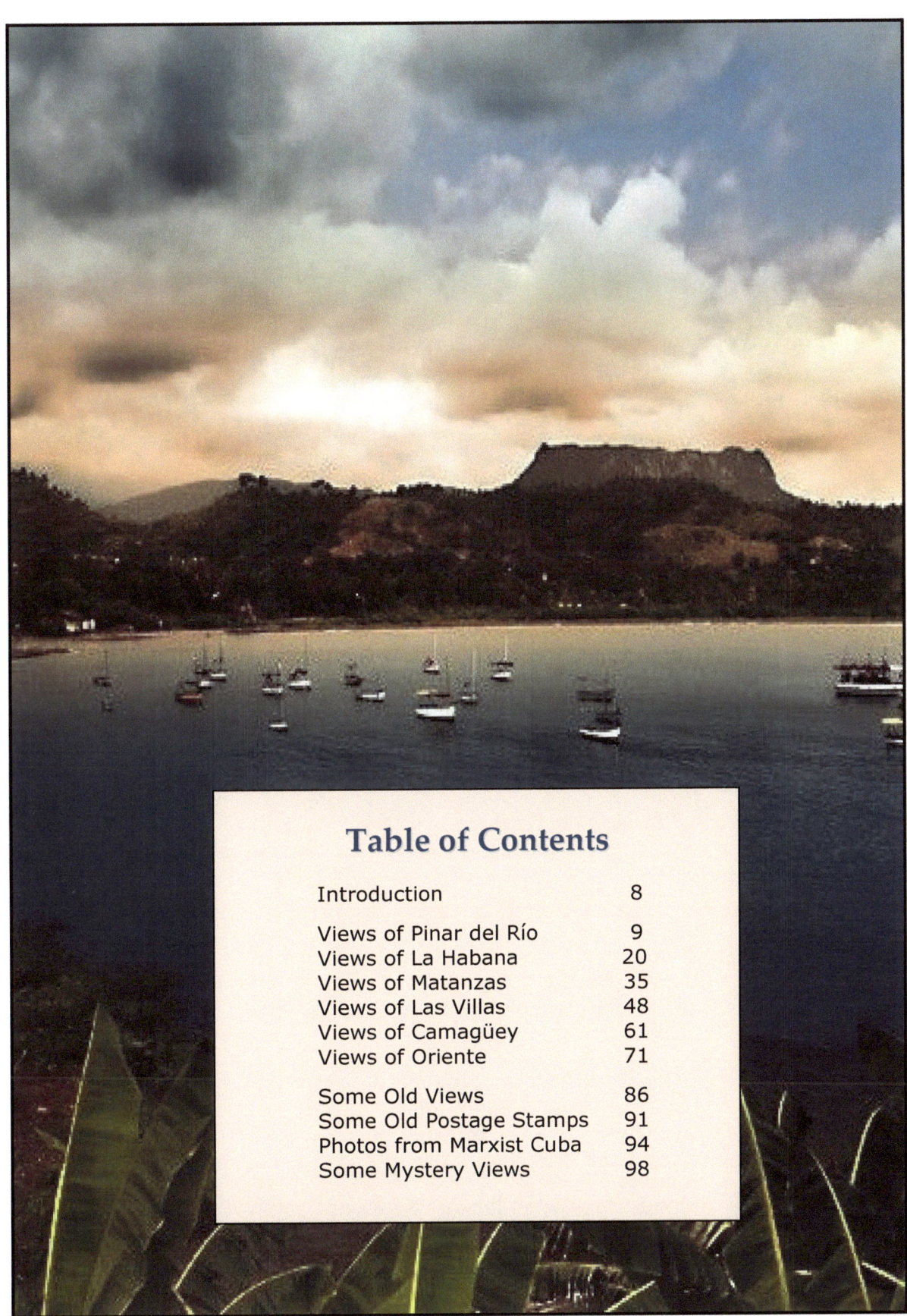

Table of Contents

Introduction	8
Views of Pinar del Río	9
Views of La Habana	20
Views of Matanzas	35
Views of Las Villas	48
Views of Camagüey	61
Views of Oriente	71
Some Old Views	86
Some Old Postage Stamps	91
Photos from Marxist Cuba	94
Some Mystery Views	98

Photo: **El Yunque**, an 1890 ft-high mountain located 4.4 miles west of Baracoa and the Baracoa Bay in Cuba's Oriente Province.

Introduction

From stunning monuments and majestic mountains, through exquisite beaches, fragrant cigars, and incredibly nice people, you can and should salsa your way from a colorful capital to the rest of the most beautiful island of the American continent, and surround yourself with history, music, beauty, splendor, character and mojitos, in one of the world's most unique places in the world, the seductive island of Cuba.

Enjoy the fresh mountain air of the **Soroa** orchidarium, the magnificence that the Creator gave the Valley of **Viñales**, the white sands and the clearest of waters in **Varadero** beach, the dramatic **Valle de los Ingenios**, the celestial inspired waterfront of **Cienfuegos**, the sea breeze of **Cayo Coco** and **Cayo Romano** in the **Jardines del Rey** Archipelago, the majestic mountains of **Sierra Maestra**, and the ancient, colossal fortifications and masterful palazzos that the Spaniards left behind.

Stroll through Havana's promenades of the **Malecón** and the **Paseo del Prado**, gazing at excellent examples of classical, Art Deco and colonial Baroque mansions, descend down to multicolored and stately caves and coves in **Bellamar** and **Sierra Cubitas**, listen to the rhythms of great orchestras and combos, playing classics, folk and jazz, choose your own corner in the two thousand miles of sandy, clear and tidy coastlines, dine on places where the DuPonts used to have dinner, listen to shows and performances once presented by Sinatra, Hope, Crosby and Brando, enjoy your own ecotour exploring rain forests, cloud forests and lagoons of all colors. Smell the refined and seductively fragranced **Mariposas**, Cuba's national flower. This is Cuba and is presented very modestly in this book.

The island of Cuba was settled 5,000 years ago. It now has the greatest diversity of marine species, trees and birds in the entire New World. Not much of what you could see there is new. Buildings, Churches, Avenues, as well as flora, fauna, land, infrastructure, institutions and resources were built over four centuries of Spanish domination and half a century of republican life. Today, Cuba lives from its past efforts and diligence, hoping that political demands do not completely spoil and destroy the island beyond repair, and before it is rescued.

We end up with some statements of past visitors and observers:

> It was Cuba, but by the signs the Indians made of its greatness, and of its gold and pearls, I thought that it must be Cipango.
> **CHRISTOPHER COLUMBUS**

> I have always looked at Cuba as the most interesting addition which could ever be made to our system of States.
> **THOMAS JEFFERSON**

> In a museum in Havana, there are two skulls of Christopher Columbus, one when he was a boy and one when he was a man.
> **MARK TWAIN**

PINAR DEL RIO

Pinar del Rio is the smallest province in Cuba, but it has coastlines on the northern and southern sides of the island; its economy is supported mostly by agriculture, and it also has an important port on the northern coastline. It also contains military bases, livestock farming, rum factories, power plants, and sugar mills. It is the westernmost province in Cuba, and it features a mountain range, fertile valleys, ample coastlines, and an archipelago. The Viñales Valley in the province was listed as a UNESCO World Heritage Site in 1999 because of the traditional tobacco-growing techniques used there. The capital of this province goes by the same name and was one of the last major cities to be founded by the Spanish in Cuba in 1867. It is the tenth-largest city in the island.

Pinar del Rio has a population of 1,485,000 persons and a surface are of 6,528 square miles.

Photos: On top, the *Guajaibón Mountains*, in the northern area of the province; the tallest peak is at 2,300 feet above sea level. Center, the *Palacio Guasch*, in the provincial capital; it is the strangest building in Cuba, built by a local doctor. It now houses a Natural Science collection. Bottom, the main *Church in Artemisa*, dedicated to its patron saint, Saint Mark the Evangelist.

Photos: On top, *Pinar del Rio's Cathedral of San Rosendo,* built in the 19th century, an eclectic temple; the façade is purely neoclassical, inside it has baroque style elements. Center, the Cathedral main altar. Below, one of the main streets of Pinar del Rio, la *Calle Real* or *Calle José Martí*.

Photos: On top, the *Gardens of Soroa,* 48 miles west of Havana, in the western region of the *Sierra del Rosario Natural Reserve Park*, and the beautiful *Soroa Falls.* Center, the *Soroa Orchids Garden*, featuring hundreds of varieties of orchids. Below, the most beautiful view in Cuba, the *Valle de Viñales*.

Photos: On top, a street in *San Juan y Martínez*, the mecca of *Vuelta Abajo*, birthplace of the finest tobacco in the world, according to purists. Center, a sunset at *Bahía Honda*, a quiet town with large rice fields around river valleys, with extensive farms and thatched roofs. Below, a view of *Mariel* from the *Loma del Vigía*, up 264 steps from the port, the original castle-residence of *Horacio Rubens*, José Martí's friend and lawyer. He gifted the castle to Cuba to be the headquarters of the country's *Naval Academy*.

Photos: On top, the Central Park of *Consolación del Sur*, known as the *Athens of Vueltabajo*, a city founded in 1690. Center, the interior of the *Teatro Milanés*, in the capital city of Pinar del Río province. It was built in 1838 and is one of the eight great theaters of colonial Cuba. Below, a tobacco farm, with its vast fields of bright green leaves of tobacco moving gently in an afternoon breeze. Pinar del Río is home to some of the most fertile lands on earth, and the world's greatest fields of premium cigar tobacco.

Photos: On top, the entrance to the *Great Cavern of Santo Tomás*, the largest cave system in Cuba and the second in the continent, with more than 29 miles in length, one of the most important hiding places of the slaves fleeing from the sugar cane plantations in colonial times. Center, *San Diego de los Baños*, a small town between the Sierra del Rosario and the Sierra de Güira; it is a natural reserve of pine, mahogany and cedar. The town has been one of the most famous Cuban seaside resorts since 1891. Below, *Maria la Gorda Beach*, in the inlet of Corrientes, in the Guanahacabibes peninsula, the dream of every scuba diving enthusiast. Its name comes from an Indigenous woman kidnapped by pirates and abandoned in this desolate place.

Photos: On top, the *Cordillera de Guaniguanico* in Pinar del Rio, formed by the subranges of Sierra del Rosario and Sierra de los Órganos. It spans 100 miles, from the town of Guane to the town of Mariel. Center, the *Peninsula de Guanahacabibes*, the sparsely populated westernmost point of Cuba. The waters surrounding it are important fishing grounds for spiny lobster and succulent red snapper. It was listed as a *Biosphere Reserve* by UNESCO in 1987. Bottom, a view of *Cabo San Antonio*, the western most point of Cuba, at the end of the Guanahacabibes Peninsula. It extends into the Yucatán Channel and is an important tourist destination.

Photos: On top, the *Cabo San Antonio*, on the Guanahacabibes Peninsula, the western extremity of Cuba. According to the International Hydrographic Organization, it marks the division point between the Caribbean Sea to the south and Gulf of Mexico to the north. Center, the *Minas de Matahambre.* Its name comes from the early 20th century when large copper reserves were discovered in the area, which represented an important source of employment for many locals. They were the deepest in the Americas at the time, and one of the most productive in the world. Below, the *Rio Cuyaguateje*, the largest and most abundant in the western region of Cuba, extending 70 miles, from its source in the Cordillera de Guaniguanico, flowing into the Ensenada de Cortés to the Caribbean Sea. It has several underground sections, within the predominantly karst geography of its course; which has given it its name.

Photos: On top, *Bahia Honda*, in northern Pinar del Rio, an area where lots of research has been done on Aboriginal peoples. It has interesting archaeological sites such as the Cuevas del Perico, del Carenero, and Felipe. Center, *Fishing at La Coloma beach,* a settlement, founded in 1607 and used by the Spanish Empire as a shipyard, due to its natural harbor. In the early 1900s, Spaniards began immigrating to Cuba, with some, mostly Galicians, settling in La Coloma in the 1930s, during the Great Depression. Below, the *Pan de Azúcar*, a mountainous relief located in the western zone of the Cordillera de Guaniguanico, 6.2 miles from the Viñales valley, with an altitude of 945 feet above sea level.

Photos: On top, *the town of Viñales*, in an area that was the home of a remnant Taíno population swelled with runaway slaves. The area was colonized at the beginning of the 1800s by tobacco growers from the Canary Islands, who settled in the Vuelta Abajo region. The first colonial settlement in Viñales dates from 1871, and the town was established in 1878, with church, school, hospital and recreation park. Center, the *Church of San Luis*, a community living mainly on agriculture (tobacco, rice, fruit crops), and stock raising. It was founded in 1827, and established as a municipality in 1879, when it split from San Juan y Martínez. Its territory includes the seaport village of La Coloma. Below, la *Cueva de San Miguel*, located in the Valley of San Vicente, 2.5 miles from Viñales. This beautiful subterranean enclave has the singular attraction of having been the first staging of the escape and settlement of the Cimaroons (escaped slaves) in the caves of the mountains.

LA HABANA

La Habana is Cuba's most populous province and also the location of the nation's capital of the same name, which is spelled in English as Havana. La Habana was one of the original six provinces into which the island was divided in 1878, but now is the largest of two areas where the original province was split in two in 2010. Except for a few small hills, its territory is flat.

The focal point of the province is the city of Havana, the capital of Cuba. It is the main port and commercial hub of the country, as well as the home of the Cuban government. The city is known for its interesting history, culture, and colorful buildings, making it a popular tourist destination, with more than one million tourists visiting every year.

The province of La Habana includes Isla de Pinos, which is the second-largest island in Cuba and has a special municipality status. The capital city of Isla de Pinos is Nueva Gerona. Much of the island is covered with citric trees and pine forests, with this last supporting its lumber industry.

The province of La Habana has a population of 2,220,000 and covers a territory of 1,225 square miles.

Photos: On top, the entrance to *Havana harbor* under a heavy storm. Havana was fortified by the Spaniards in the XVI century, after the Crown transferred the governor's residence to Havana from Santiago de Cuba, on the eastern end of the island in 1553. It made Havana the *de facto* capital. Center, the portal of the old *Palace of the Spanish Captain Generals* in Havana. This Baroque-style mansion was built in the 1770s and fills the entire western side of the city's Plaza de Armas. The gorgeous courtyard is full of trees and peacocks. Below, a view of the *National Capitol* on Prado Avenue in Havana. The tall building on the left is the *National Telephone Company* on Dragones Street.

MEMORIES 21

Photos: On top, one of the towers of the *Centro Gallego* in Havana, located on the *Paseo del Prado*, a boulevard that straddles a good part of Old Havana; this building stands and wraps around the structure where the *Teatro Tacón* was built in 1838. Below, the *Plaza in front of the old Havana Cathedral, and the Cathedral main altar*. This temple is one of eleven Catholic Cathedrals on the island. It is located in the Plaza de la Catedral on Calle Empedrado, between San Ignacio y Mercaderes, in Old Havana. The 100 by 130 feet rectangular church serves as the seat of the Roman Catholic Archdiocese of San Cristóbal de la Habana. Christopher Columbus' remains were kept in the Cathedral between 1796 and 1898 before they were taken to Seville after Cuba's independence.

Photos: at the Top, the *Paseo del Prado*, starting at the *Fraternity Park* and ending at the entrance of Havana Bay, right across from El Morro. Construction of this magnificent boulevard was the first thoroughfare outside the city walls, and was completed in the mid-1830s during the term of Captain General Miguel Tacón. In 1925, French landscape architect Jean-Claude Nicolas Forestier redesigned it by lining it with trees, bronze sculptures of lions, coral stone walls and marble benches. Center, the façade of the *National Capitol* and the *Centro Gallego* on the Paseo del Prado. Below, the *Templete*, a neo-classical old church and monument celebrating the first mass in San Cristóbal de la Habana, which took place on November 16, 1519. Its interior has paintings by Jean Baptiste Vermay, the founding director of Havana's Academia Nacional de Bellas Artes San Alejandro in 1818.

Photos: Three views of the *Universidad de la Habana*, founded on January 5, 1728; it is the oldest in Cuba, and one of the first to be founded in the Americas. Top and Center, the *monumental steps* built in 1927, and the statue of the *Alma Mater* at the end of the 88 steps; Below, the University's impressive *Aula Magna*, a dazzling neoclassic and baroque room holding in a marble urn the remains of the Cuban philosopher and priest Félix Varela. The University was founded by Dominican friars as the *Real y Pontificia Universidad de San Gerónimo de la Habana,* with six faculties: Art and Philosophy, Theology, Canons, Law, and Medicine. In 1842, it became a secular, royal and literary institution, and its name changed to the *Real y Literaria Universidad de La Habana*. Later, after Cuba's independence, the name was changed to *University of Havana*.

Photos: Three views of Havana's *Central Park,* the social, political and cultural epicenter of Havana, with pink slabs and stately palms. On top, the *Centro Asturiano*, a beautiful palace of white stone, rich marbles and irons, erected by the efforts of 61,000 Asturian immigrants to Cuba, with a design based on the *Palacio de Comunicaciones* in Madrid; it was inaugurated in 1927. Below, on the left, the *Hotel Inglaterra*, seat of the *Acera del Louvre,* were Cuban patriots used to assemble to conspire in the 1800s. Finally, *on the bottom right,* the magnificent statue of *José Martí*, the Apostol of Cuban independence, erected 10 years after his death.

Photos: Three views of the *Cuban National Presidential Palace* in Havana, inaugurated in 1920 by President Mario García Menocal. On top, the building itself, at Refugio Street between Monserrate and Zulueta Streets. Below, two views of the artistic *ceiling frescos*, by *Armando García Menocal, Leopoldo Romañach, Antonio Rodríguez Morey, Esteban Valderrama, Mariano Miguel González, y Juan Emilio Hernández Giró*. The building was designed by the Cuban architect Rodolfo Maruri, and the Belgian architect Paul Belau, who also designed the Centro Gallego, The Presidential Palace was inaugurated in 1920 by President Mario García Menocal. The building has Neo-Classical elements and was decorated by Tiffany Studios of New York City.

Photos: On this page, three views in Havana. On top, the *entrance to the Barrio Chino* (Chinatown). The Chinese came to Cuba after 1857 to work in the sugar fields; they fought in the Cuban Wars of Independence, but many of them left Cuba after the Marxist revolution of 1959. Center left, the *Necropolis of Colón*, one of the richest in the world, with hundreds of marble statuary. Below right, the area under the dome of the *National Capitol*, with a bronze statue of the Republic; at 56 ft in height, the third tallest indoors sculpture in the Americas. The building was commissioned by Cuban president Gerardo Machado and built from 1926 to 1929 under the direction of Eugenio Rayneri Piedra. It is located on the city block at Paseo del Prado, Dragones, Industria, and San José streets, in what at the time was the exact center of Havana.

Photos: On top, the ballroom of the *Casino Español in Havana*, one of the eight Casinos Españoles built in Colonial Cuba: *Havana* (1869), *Sagua la Grande* (1871), *Colón* (1881), *Remedios* (1884), *Placetas* (1885), *Cruces* (1888), *Matanzas* (1899) and *Santa Clara* (1899). Bottom left, the *Hotel Nacional de Cuba*, a historic Spanish eclectic style hotel, opened in 1930 on Taganana Hill in the Vedado district. It offers commanding views of the sea and the city. From the garden you can see two of the Santa Clara Battery cannons from the Defense System of Havana during the Spanish colonial period. Bottom right, the *Monument in honor of José Martí*, located on the northern side of the *Plaza Cívica,* built in 1958. It is a 360 ft. star-shaped tower, at which base is an enormous 55 ft tall statue of Martí, carved on site from white marble from Isla de Pinos, sitting and deep in thought. It is the largest monument to a writer anywhere in the world.

Photos: Above, three important places in Havana: the *Bacardí Building*, a landmark completed in 1930 on the corner of Calles Monserrate and San Juan de Dios. It was designed to be the headquarters for the Bacardi Rum Company. Its interiors are famous for their many original decorations in marble and granite, and it is regarded as one of the finest Art Deco buildings in Latin America. Below left, the *Monument in Honor of Máximo Gómez*, erected along the Paseo de Malecón in 1935. This equestrian monument by sculptor Aldo Gamba shows Cuba's hero facing the sea. Beneath its marble platform supported by a dozen columns, is a bas-relief fronted by the winged Victoria, the Roman goddess of victory in war. Bottom right, the *Plaza and Convent of San Francisco*, built in 1628 and 1591, respectively. The plaza is one of the oldest public squares in the Americas. It is named after the Franciscan Convent built on its side. A market was historically held in this square for over a hundred years, and was eventually moved to the *Plaza Vieja de La Habana* as the monks from the church complained of the noise.

Photos: On top, the interior and the façade of the *Iglesia de la Merced*, a church with an austere exterior and a beautiful interior, begun in 1755, and completed in the 19th century, with late-baroque and early neoclassical elements. It has its own small square, and Havana's most sumptuous ecclesiastical interior, beautiful, gilded altars, frescoed vaults and a number of valuable old paintings, plus a quiet cloister on its side. Below, left, is the monumental (66 ft high plus a 10 ft base, weighting 320 tons) sculpture of the *Cristo de La Habana*, placed in a Casablanca hilltop overlooking the bay. It was carved out of white Carrara marble, brought from Italy after being personally blessed by the Pope. The statue was left with empty eyes to give the impression of looking at people wherever they are. Due to the position of its hands, people say that he holds a *cigar* in his right arm and a *mojito* on the left. Finally, below right, the *Virgen del Camino*, at a small park in the intersection of roads that lead to *Cotorro, Regla, Guanabacoa, San José de las Lajas, San Miguel del Padrón* and *Arroyo Naranjo*. The statue, the brainchild of Rita Longa, was blessed by Cardinal Arteaga, who consecrated her as "*protective mother of the pilgrim traveler*," a designation encouraged and blessed by the Holy See.

Photos: Above, the entrance to the *Escolapios de Guanabacoa*, the first institutional presence of the Piarist Fathers in the American continent, following the requests of Saint Anthony Mary Claret and the Queen of Spain Isabel II. At the center, the entrance to the *Tunnel of Calle Linea*, connecting the Capital of Havana, under the Rio Almendares, with the municipality of Marianao. Linea street got its name by having the first rail ways for trains and street cars in metropolitan Havana. Below, the park across from the *Lonja del Comercio* in Havana, shown at the left. The Lonja, founded in 1909, served as the stock exchange in the capital until the Marxists confiscated it. Its design is a mixed Renaissance and eclectic style.

Photos: Top to Bottom, the *Colegio de La Salle del Vedado*, a symbol of Cuban education and architectural splendor in times of the Republic, an imposing five-story building, located on Calle 13, between B and C, in the Havana neighborhood of el Vedado. Center, the *Maternidad Obrera Hospital*, inaugurated in 1941; its imposing architecture is among the most important exponents of Art Deco in the city of Havana. It received the Gold Medal Award of the National College of Architects in 1942. Below, the *Havana Carnival*. It has been celebrated for centuries in memory of the slaves who would recreate the songs and dances of their homeland on the feat of Corpus Christy, around the 6th of January.

Photos: On top, *Cojimar*, a town that is part of Habana del Este. Its population is 20,390. It was an inspiration for Ernest Hemingway's 1952 novel *The Old Man and the Sea,* which is based on a real story in 1940s, when an enormous great white shark was caught; it was one of the contenders for the largest specimen of all time. Center, *Melena del Sur*, a town and a municipality located south of Havana Province. It is bordered on the north and northwest by San José de las Lajas, on the east by Güines, and on the west by Batabanó and the Gulf of Batabanó. There are several versions regarding the meaning of the name *Melena*, from the Greek *Melaine* (black), which is the predominant color of some of its most fertile land. Below, the *Parque de Santiago de Las Vegas;* the first city settlement dates from 1683 when tobacco farmers worked on the lands of the ranches in Sócalo Hondo, Managua, Bejucal and La Chorrera. In 1824, the town was declared a city, and their people raised a statue of the Spanish King Ferdinand VII, who corresponded by granting the city the title of *Faithful and Very Illustrious*.

Photos: On top, the lobby of the *Marques de San Felipe y Santiago de Bejucal*, a Hotel in the Plaza de San Francisco in La Habana, honoring a Grande of Spain, and sharing its name with the town of *Bejucal*, which borders with the towns of Boyeros, San José de las Lajas, Quivicán and San Antonio de los Baños, near the capital of Havana. Center, the *Ariguanabo River*, a stream in San Antonio de los Baños, in Havana province, which goes underground at a cave in the center of town, and is literarily threatening to disappear. Below, a view of a coastal pond in the *Isla de Pinos*, the largest (850 square miles) island in Cuban waters. Historically, it was home to the Siboney Indians, who left there one of the most important collections of rock art throughout Cuba, especially in the *Punta del Este Caves*.

Matanzas is the second-largest province in Cuba and is one of the most industrialized. In addition to sugar production, petroleum products play a significant role in the region's economy. The capital is also named Matanzas, and it's known for being a cultural center, the *Atenas of Cuba*. There are seventeen bridges crossing three rivers in the city of Matanzas, which give it the nickname, City of Bridges.

The province of Matanzas has a total population of 717,000 persons and covers a territory of 4,553 square miles.

Photos: On top, the *Parque de la Libertad* in Matanzas. a place intended for recreation, conversation, or walking, where a wide variety of cultural activities often take place. This was the Plaza de Armas built in 1800, a place where patriots conspired against the Spanish army. In the center stand two statues, Liberty and José Martí, that represent the most important sculpture group in the city, created by the Italian sculptor Buemi and inaugurated in 1909. According to tradition, Liberty, on the base of the monument is screaming: "*I am hungry...*" and Martí, at the top, is pointing to his left, saying "*Go to the Louvre*...[a famous eatery]." At the center, the *Teatro Sauto,* a favorite of Caruso for its acoustics; it is one of the three main Classical theaters in Cuba, located on the south side of the *Plaza de la Vigía Square* of Matanzas, with an impressive profile that dominates the entire area. Below, an aerial view of the city and some of its rivers and bridges.

Photos: A view of the famous *Cuevas de Bellamar*, dating back 300,000 years, one of the natural treasures of Cuba, discovered in 1861; inside you will find *helictites*, solid calcite crystals hanging from *stalactites*, only found there, which have attracted the attention of geologists from all over the world, as well as many remains of birds and vertebrates from the Quaternary Period. On the left, the *Matanzas Cathedral of San Carlos Borromeo*, a neoclassical structure with two unequal towers founded in 1693. On the right, the beautiful and elegant *main altar of the Cathedral*, surrounded by frescoes on the walls, ceilings and a grandiose big dome.

Photos: On top, two images of the world renown *Playa de Varadero*, whose crystalline waters and fine sand extend east of the city of Matanzas for more than 13 miles. In the center, the *Plaza de la Vigía*, the old Plaza de Armas founded in 1693; the entire city of Matanzas was built around it. The statue is dedicated to Col. Alberto Schweyer Lamar, Chief Medical Officer of General Pedro Betancourt. Below, the *Teatro Velasco*, opened in 1916, and named after hotelier Luis Zorrilla Velasco. It was there that the first movie shot in Cuba, *Simulacro de Incendio* (Fire Drill), lasting no more than a minute, began the history of cinema in Cuba. The building survives today screening films from America and Cuba.

Photos: On top, the *Cárdenas Cathedral*, dated from the XIX century, a single hall church with a superb hardwood ceiling, a tall iron dome, large stained-glass windows, and a beautiful classic arc that leads to the altar. Below, two views of *Cárdenas*, the 15th largest city in Cuba and, after Manzanillo, the second most populated city not being a provincial seat. The Cuban Flag was first raised in Cuba in this historic city of straight and narrow streets, horse-drawn carriages, industry and "*cangrejos*" (blue crabs). Cárdenas is as traditional and simple, as Varadero is modern and glamorous. The city of Cárdenas preserves traditional values and the essence of a republican Cuba of years past. It is an unforgettable place, beautiful, with dribs and drabs of Colonial buildings and 19th century arches splashed across the city. It preserves the untouchable magic of an indescribable age and good times, which surround the place like a perpetual mist.

Photos: On top, the *Ciénaga de Zapata*, a territory in the southern side of Matanzas province with many ecosystems, from mangrove forests, seagrass beds, coral reef barriers, and an underwater canyon, with large groups of high-backed snappers and groupers. It covers 75% of the Zapata Peninsula, and is an exotic marshy area of almost 1930 square miles, considered one of the most interesting corners of Cuba; a well-preserved wetland with very low population. A wide variety of fauna and flora is found there; due to the humidity of the area and the soil, the American crocodiles, have made their home in Zapata. On the left, one of the pristine *caves near Varadero beach*. Below, the *Bueyvaquita Beach*, around 0.14 miles in length, extremely popular although super small; its fame is due to its incredibly transparent waters.

Photos: On top, the *Church of San Pedro Apóstol* in Versalles, a neighborhood in the city of Matanzas. This is one of the neoclassical style buildings that adorn Matanzas. It was designed by Daniel Dall Aglio, the same architect of the *Teatro Sauto*, and it is main nave imitates the Vatican's with a barrel vault dome and grooves on the sides and, at the intersection, another small dome. Two towers on each side of the nave provide the building with perfect symmetry. Center, the old *Triolet Pharmacy of Matanzas,* one of the best preserved in the world, founded in 1882 by Dr. Triolet Lelievre, a native of Lissy, and resident of Sagua la Grande, north of Las Villas. Below, the *Instituto de Matanzas*, inaugurated in 1864, located in the city block limited by Dos de Mayo, Milanés, Contreras and América streets. It was famous for its academic excellence and its sports tradition.

Photos: On top, the *Ermita de Monserrate*, a Spanish-style Church on a Matanzas hilltop offering beautiful views of the city and the Yumurí Valley. On the right, the 8 feet *Bronze Monument to Cristobal Colón*, with him leaning on an anchor, pointing to the newly discovered land. On the base the word: *Tierra*. Below, The *San Severino Fort in Matanzas*, the oldest building in the city, of marked similarity to the Fuerza Castle of Havana, though it exceeds its mobility and defensive capabilities. Finally, the *San Miguel de los Baños Hotel and Resort*, built in 1929, offering bathing and drinking the area's sulfur water, which has long been thought to have natural health benefits. San Miguel has been very popular in the United States and Europe.

Photos: On top, a view of one of the many *bridges of Matanzas city*. The economic development fostered by the sugar industry in the 19th century favored the multiplication of neighborhoods, and with them the crossings over the waters; today, thirty bridges make it possible for *Matanceros* to go across the city. Center, the *Fort of La Loma*, in Colón, Matanzas, built by the Spaniards in the 19th century in the midst of the war for Cuba's national independence. It was originally baptized with the official name of *Alfonso XIII Fort*. Below, a *wide view of Matanzas* from the Church of San Pedro in Versailles.

Photos: On top. The interior of the *Teatro Sauto*. It can house up to 775 spectators, and has a rounded stage that when lifted converts the auditorium into a ballroom. It has a Neoclassical style, predominantly the Greek Ionic and Doric classical order. Center, the *Valle del Yumurí,* where you can see in the mountains the profile of a sleeping Indian. Legend has it that a cacique brought a magical fish to Matanzas as a gift, which a young woman ate; she lay down to sleep and never waked up. The area where she was resting was transformed into a mountain, preserving the figure of the sleeping girl. The mountain was later named the *Pan de Matanzas*. Below, the *Palacio de Justicia* de Matanzas, located in the central Plaza de la Vigía; it was built in 1826 as the customs building, today it has become the Palace of Justice or Provincial Court.

Photos: On top, the *Cienaga de Zapata*, the largest municipality of Cuba with 1606 square miles, and quite a few villages, a most valuable natural reservoir that stands out nationally, regionally and worldwide. It has an extensive variety of ecosystems, mainly in zones where the saltwater-freshwater interphase, with around 900 autochthonous plant species, grouped into 110 families, 115 of which are endemics. Center, the *Laguna del Tesoro*, accessed by boat through a channel surrounded by lush vegetation. This lake has an area of 3.5 square miles, and 0.65 miles in diameter, with plenty of trout in its crystalline waters. According to legend, the Indigenous people, fearing the Spanish conquistadors, sank a boat full of their most precious possessions in the lake to avoid the theft of their riches. Below, *Río Canimar*, a Natural Park with exhuberant vegetation, where you can ride a horse, swim in its waters and later snorkel in one of the most famous caves in Cuba, the *Cueva de Saturno*.

Photos: On top, a view of the *Gran Parque Natural Montemar Biosphere Reserve* in the Ciénaga de Zapata National Park. The ecological fragility of its ecosystems has led to an intense effort toward conserving biodiversity and natural resources. The region was established as a UNESCO Biosphere Reserve, and it remains one of the Caribbean's most untamed, least inhabited regions. It is not shocking that the Ciénaga de Zapata has gained worldwide renown as a birdwatching region. In this region only, visitors can find the *Cuban Bee Hummingbird*, the world's smallest bird. Center, the *Escuela de Artes y Oficios de Colón*, founded in 1912, offering classes in Cutting and Sewing, Cooking and Dietetics, Modeling and Plastic, Soap and Perfume making, Mechanical workshops, Foundry and Carpentry, considered one of the best in Cuba. Below, *San Miguel de los Baños Gran Hotel y Balneario*, modeled after the Grand Casino in Monte Carlo, at one time the top destination for wealthy vacationers visiting Cuba for baths fed by natural springs. In the 1950's, pollution from sugar mills contaminated the water and forced it to be abandoned. Today, the glorious Gran Hotel y Balneario sits empty.

Photos: On top, *Cárdenas*, where the Cuban Flag was first raised over Cuba; a historic city of straight and narrow streets (the "*Charleston of the Caribbean*"), horse-drawn carriages, industry, and "*cangrejos*" (blue crabs). It was there where José Arechabala launched the production of Havana Club in 1934. Center, the *Puente de la Concordia*, inaugurated in 1878; it was built to connect the neighborhoods of Versalles and Matanzas, separated by the Yumurí River. It is a work of art, considered by many specialists in the field as one of the most beautiful structures of the time. The iron structure on which it rests was forged in the United States. Below, *Versailles Quarter*, a picturesque place dating back to 1827, when it was called *Yumurí* in honor of the river passing through the area. It received its French name in 1850, due to the French populating the area at that time. Versailles, throughout the 19th century, was the place of leisure for the upper-class families of Matanzas.

LAS VILLAS

Las Villas is a province in central Cuba with the capital city of Santa Clara. Sugar and tobacco are its two important commodities; the construction of beach resorts on its northern coastline has turned the region in a prosperous money mecca from tourism.

Santa Clara was founded in 1689 and is presently Cuba's fifth-most populous city. It is the location of the iconic Parque Vidal. A most important city is Cienfuegos, located in central western Cuba along the country's southern coast; it was named after the Captain General of Cuba from 1816-1819, José Cienfuegos. The city has played a significant role in the country's sugar industry for many decades. Sugar mills are located throughout the region and growing, and processing sugar have always been major economic activities

Two other important cities are Sancti Spíritus, and Trinidad. The province has Cuba's largest man-made reservoir, the Embalse Zaza. Sugar cane and cattle are two important contributors to the region's economy, and the old and well recognized city of Trinidad is also a major tourist attraction. It's listed as a UNESCO World Heritage Site and is full of colonial buildings that date back to the 16th century.

The province of Las Villas has a population of 1,600,000 persons, and a total area of 6,037 square miles.

Photos: Three views of Santa Clara, the landlocked capital of the Las Villas province; it is situated near the geographic center of the island, on the country's Central Highway, and is the junction point of Cuba's main rail lines. It was founded in 1689 by families fleeing constant pirate threats in coastal Remedios, and occupies the site of the ancient Indian town of *Cubanacán*, which, according to authorities, Christopher Columbus mistook for the city of the Mongol emperor *Kublai Khan*. At the top and center, the *Plaza de Santa Clara* and *Marta Abreu University*, Cuba's third-biggest center of high studies. As seen in the bottom image, Santa Clara is home to countess *examples of colonial aristocratic living conditions*.

Photos: Above, the *Teatro La Caridad de Santa Clara,* one of the most relevant cultural places in this province and Cuba; it has seen world-renowned figures and companies parading through its stage. Below, two photos of *Parque Leoncio Vidal,* the square where you find the *Teatro La Caridad*; the park, formerly known as "*Plaza de Recreo,*" owes its name to the Cuban patriot *Leoncio Vidal*, who died in a military action in 1896. In the 1930s, the park was the scene of protests and demonstrations by students, workers and the population in general. For centuries, *Parque Vidal* has been present in the sad as well as happy memories of numerous generations.

Photos: On top, *The Cathedral of Santa Clara de Assis*, on calle Marta Abreu, one of the city's main arteries; on its right, its main altar. It replaced in 1940 the original old *Cathedral or Iglesia Mayor* built in 1738. For over 30 years, the *Virgen del Camino* (see page 24) was lost after the revolution removed it from its place in Havana. In 1995, it was found in a ditch and the people of Santa Clara claimed it, since it had originally been in Santa Clara. Below, the *Cathedral of San Juan de los Remedios*; on its left, its main altar. Remedios is the third oldest city in Cuba, founded in 1514 by *Vasco Porcallo de Figueroa*. Vasco was married to a daughter of the *Cacique of Sabaneque* and to avoid taxes, Vasco hid his founding of the city for many years. In 1672, Remedios was declared a city possessed by Satan and most of its inhabitants moved north, founding the city of Santa Clara. Luckily, enough people stayed in Remedios.

Photos: Three important images from *The Palacio del Valle* in the city of Cienfuegos; it is a historic mansion built by the Italian architect, Alfredo Colli, from 1913 to 1917, with Carrara marble, Italian alabaster, Venetian and Granada ceramics, Spanish ironwork and forges, Talavera mosaics and European crystals; the woodworks are all mahogany from Cuba. Its style has Gothic, Romanesque, Baroque and Italianate influences, combined with the Mudejar style that was in vogue in Spain in the 12th and 13th centuries. It is located in *Punta Gorda*, and for years it has housed a restaurant and terrace bar, hosting frequent cultural events.

Photos: Views from probably the most beautiful places in Las Villas Province. On top and center, two photos of the *Cienfuegos Tennis and Yacht Club* in Punta Gorda, a private Club and Marina for the ultra-wealthy, facing the Malecón near *Punta Gorda*. Below, a photo of *El Nicho Natural Park,* a waterfall surrounded by green everywhere; it is the jewel of an area between Cienfuegos and Trinidad known as the *Pocetas de Cristal.*

Photos: On top: *Potrerillo falls* in *Topes de Collantes* (Collantes' Highs), near San Juan peak, the highest elevation (3,740 ft) in the Escambray Mountains range, which faces the bulk of *Villa Clara Province* to the north, *and the cities of Cienfuegos* to the west, and *Sancti Spiritus* to the east. On the left, a night view of *Sancti Spíritus,* a town that during the 17th century, was attacked by both Dutch and British pirates, in both cases with little success thanks to its impressive Spanish garrison. On the bottom, *a view of the Rio Jatibonico,* a native name derived from *hati* (wood) and *bonico* (area), a place of extensive forests.

Photos: On top, a view of the *Escambray Mountains*, in the central region of Cuba, straddling the areas around the cities of Sancti Spíritus, Cienfuegos and Santa Clara, extending 50 miles from east to west, and 50 from north to south. On the right, the *City of Trinidad*, a UNESCO World Heritage site. On the bottom, the *Jesuit Church and School in Sagua la Grande*, one of the few Gothic style churches in Cuba, with a remarkably famous and learned school at its side. The church tower is the highest point in the city and can be seen on the side of the *Puente del Triunfo*, and from anywhere in town.

Photos: On top. Cubans revere the well-known Viñales Valley, one of Cuba's most iconic natural landscapes. 175 miles east of Havana, however, the municipality of Sagua la Grande has as impressive a set of important views as Viñales: the *Mogotes de Jumagua*, eight precious mounds, preceded by a splendid palm grove. It is a National Ecological Reserve and an identity symbol of Sagua, la Villa del Undoso. At the center, a beautiful 1912 Neoclassical building, Las Villas' *Provincial Government,* housing the *José Martí Library*, one of the most beautiful buildings of Santa Clara on the eastern part of Leoncio Vidal Park. Below, the *Parque Leoncio Vidal* at night. Its name comes from the Cuban patriot **Leoncio Vidal Caro**, who died there fighting in 1896 in what was then known as "***Plaza de Recreo***" (Recreation Square). It has many historical monuments: a replica of the Eiffel Tower, a 1911 *Glorieta*, a place for musical ensembles to delight residents, a bronze statue of Marta Abreu, a bust of Colonel Leoncio Vidal, and *La Farola,* which marks the place where Vidal fell fighting and died.

Photos: On top, *Caibarién*, located on the north coast of Las Villas in central Cuba, was founded in 1841. The name comes from Cayo Barien, its first name; it is a village with a tradition of fishing and fresh sea breeze all year round. Center, The *Pedraplén*, the largest causeway in the world, linking Cuba with kilometers of amazing, untouched beaches of golden and fine white sand, and crystalline turquoise waters, among them Las Brujas, Ensenachos, Perla Blanca, Santa María and Mégano, all with lush vegetation and amazing landscapes. Below, *Cayo Las Brujas*, the first thing you find when you cross the *Pedraplén* which connects the island of Cuba with the rest of the keys of the archipelago known as Cayerías del Norte.

Photos: On top, the iron bridge *El Triunfo*, built in Sagua la Grande when the original wooden bridge was destroyed during a flood of the Undoso River. Under the openwork lace of its sidewalks, the waters run slowly, the shores are strewn with boats, and the city takes a certain port nuance. Crossing it, one arrives at Martí Street, where Sagua la Grande was first settled. Center, *Isabela de Sagua*, founded in 1843 as the port and customs of Sagua, and located in front of the *Jardines del Rey* archipelago. Known as *La Venecia de Cuba*, it is a village of the municipality of Sagua la Grande. It has been severely damaged by hurricanes, but its nearly 3,000 residents refuse to move inland, giving the hamlet the fame of "*the city that resists to die.*" Below, *Camajuani at night*, a town founded in 1864. Its name means "crystal waters." When Ferrocarriles Unidos de Caibarién built a station on the *Hacienda Camajuaní*, the place became a town and took its name. Sometimes it seems like time stands still here, except every year in March, during the *Parrandas*, fiestas that combine music, dance, visual arts and fireworks, and constitute one of the most beautiful shows in Cuba.

Photos: On top, the Central Park of *Quemado de Güines*, founded in 1667, bordering Corralillo, Sagua la Grande and Santo Domingo. Its founders were several families of woodcutters who, in order to colonize the area to begin logging, started by burning its abundant trees, hence its name. On its left, the *Guajirigallo de Quemado de Güines*. It is a *porrón* with the head of a *guajiro* and the spurs and tail of a *rooster*. The peasantry, dedicated to agricultural work, used to get up with the song of the rooster, and leave to work with an inseparable companion, a porrón to quench their thirst. Below, the *Parque Marti de Cruces*, a town founded in 1852 in a place known as *Sabana de Ibarra*. Here the Battle of Bad Weather (La Batalla de Mal Tiempo), was fought on December 15, 1895. Cuban rebels engaged Spanish troops, setting fire to the sugarcane fields and charging the Spanish with machetes. The Cubans reported 4 dead and 4 wounded, inflicting 200 casualties, capturing 150 Mausers, 60 Remingtons, 6 boxes of ammunition, horses, first aid supplies, and flags and documents of the Spaniards.

Photos: On top, the *City Hall of Ranchuelo*, a town founded in 1734, originally named Boca de Ranchuelo; it is 27 miles from Santa Clara and 160 from Havana. Center, a scene from the *town of Cifuentes*, founded in 1819, south of Sagua la Grande, with a large population of descendants of people born in the Canary Islands, who brought knowledge for tobacco plantations with them. Below, a view of the *Sierra del Escambray*. The range is divided in two by the Agabama River. The western part is called the Guamuhaya Mountains, and the eastern part, raising between Trinidad and Sancti Spiritus, is the Sierra de Sancti Spíritus. In the southeastern range of the Escambray, is Topes de Collantes, a nature reserve park full of caves, rivers, waterfalls, and canyons, and the Valle de los Ingenios, a UNESCO World Heritage Site.

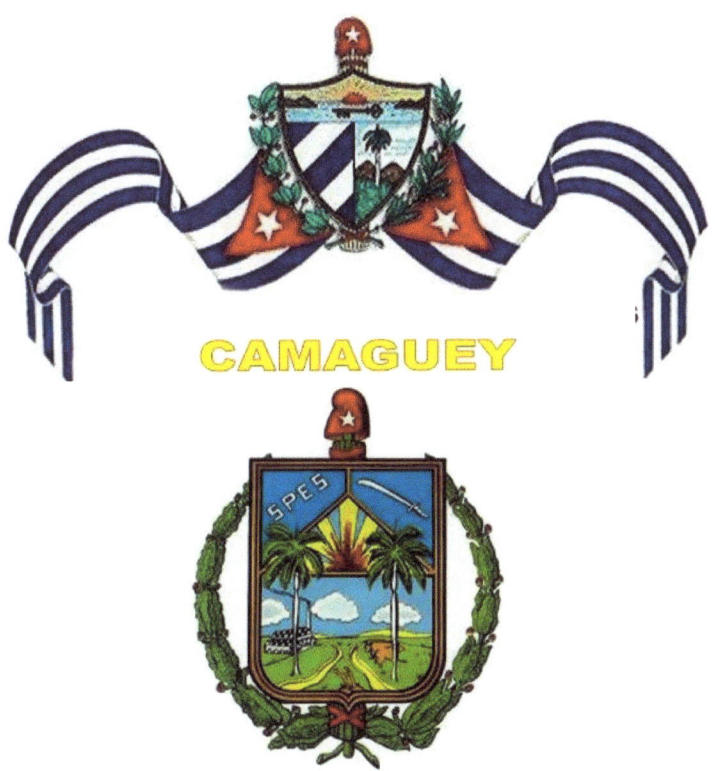

Camagüey is the largest of the Cuban provinces, though it does not have the highest population. The capital of Camagüey goes by the same name as the province, and two other notable cities are Florida and Nuevitas. The province has two coastlines, one on each side of the island, both with excellent beaches. The northern coast features two archipelagos, the southern coast several cays.

There are no mountains or large hills in this province. Its economy is mostly supported by sugar and cattle production. The province is home to Laguna de Leche, Cuba's largest natural lake, and there are many mangroves on the province's southern coast. An important economic activity is the production of pineapple and citrus fruits.

One other main city is Ciego de Ávila, which was founded in 1840. It lies on the Carretera Central highway of Cuba and is crossed by a major railroad. There are several impressive colonial Spanish buildings in the city's center.

Camagüey has a total population of 1,120,000 persons, and a surface area of 8,633 square miles.

Photos: On the top, a second story terrace at *Avenida de los Mártires* in Camagüey, a kilometer long showcase of premium buildings with beautiful column façades. In the 19th century, this avenue was a rural road that passed in front of the Cavalry Barracks of the City of Port-au-Prince, one of the main Spanish military strongholds in the area. Today it is an important avenue with two tracks on each side of a green median that holds a row of tall, discreet and elegant lighting poles. Center, *La Cueva de los Portales*, in the *Sierra de Cubitas*, an important orographic group with caves, sinkholes, fissures, and underground streams of incomparable beauty, with Indo-Cuban cave paintings. Below, *La Laguna de la Leche* in Morón, the largest natural lake in Cuba, with a surface of 25.5 square miles; its limestone sediments give it the milky name, due to the fresh-and-salty composition of its water.

Photos: On top, a typical *garden* with *tinajones*, a scene you will see in most every city in Camagüey. At the center, two images of the *Camagüey Cemetery*, the oldest in operation in Cuba; it was planned in 1790 and opened in 1814, and it is worth visiting, almost like the cemetery of Havana. Its origin is linked to the *Parroquia del Cristo del Buen Viaje*, erected in 1792. Below, a night view of the *Iglesia de Nuestra Señora de la Soledad*, located at a corner of República and Ignacio Agramonte streets, built during the 18th century, with Baroque frescos and the very fountain where Ignacio Agramonte was baptized in 1841.

Photos: On top, a beautiful sight at *Cayo Coco*, in Ciego de Avila, in the *Jardines del Rey* archipelago, off north central Cuba; it is known for its white-sand beaches and coral reefs. At the center, a wharf at *Cayo Romano*, the largest cay of the *Jardines del Rey*, with a total surface of 300 square miles. *Cayo Romano* is one of the best locations anywhere to catch the most combative and acrobatic species while enjoying the exclusiveness of a vast area of endless waters. Located on the north shore of the eastern province of Camaguey, the *Cayo Romano* fishery is an enormous system of flats, lagoons and pristine estuaries. Below, the top of a mountain in the *Sierra de Cubitas* chain; it was most probably there, according to researchers, where groups of *agro-potters* from the area of the Orinoco River in Venezuela first began to move to the Antillean arch at the beginning of our era. After the Spanish colonization in the 1500s, the area became an important agricultural zone throughout the coastal plain to the north of Camagüey.

Photos: On top, The *Escuelas Pías* of Camagüey, one of the oldest building in the city. It was a Convent in the XVIII century, repaired and extended by the Piarist Fathers in the 1930s. At the center, *Constitutional Park in Guaimaro*, the city where the first Cuban Constitution was signed in 1869. At the base of the monument, a bronze plaque shows pictures of José Martí, Máximo Gómez, Carlos Manuel de Céspedes, Ignacio Agramonte, Calixto García, and Antonio Maceo. Below, the *Centro Asturiano* of Ciego de Ávila, founded in 1929, confiscated and turned into a Museum in 1960.

Photos: On top, a night view of the city of *Vertientes*, about 20 miles west of the city of Camagüey. It was there that the gigantic American-owned and operated *Central Vertientes*, confiscated by the government of Cuba, was located in the center of a very fertile sugar growing region. Center, an interesting *corner in the city of Camagüey*, which people say it has all the history, architecture, and charm of more popular cities in Cuba, but none of the crowds or hassle. Below, an *aerial view of the city*. They say that the clustered streets are a direct result of the city's historical fights and its constant defense against rebel-raiders like Henry Morgan. The complicated layout was created to confuse invading pirates and provide shelter for the city's residents, who were constantly on edge from the relentless attacks.

Photos: On top, *Monument to Salvador Cisneros Betancourt, Marqués of Santa Lucía,* president of the Cuban Republic at Arms from 1873 to 1875. As a young man, he was imprisoned in Spain for his conspiratorial activities, and fought in Cuba's two wars of independence; he was president of the insurgent government in both wars. Center, *Cayo Sabinal,* embraced by the waters of the Atlantic Ocean. It has one of the most beautiful coral reefs of the world, second in size only to the Australian one, stretching west and reaching Varadero beach. It owes its name to the abundance of a tree named *Sabina* (Juniper). The mists of old legends shroud tales of corsairs and pirates stopping there in their sinister adventures for loot, commerce and smuggling. Below, an *aerial night view of Camagüey*, Cuba's third-largest city with 321,000 inhabitants, founded in 1514 as Santa María de Puerto Príncipe and moved inland in 1528, to the site of a Taino village named Camagüey.

Photos: On top, *Playa Santa Lucía*, northeast to Camagüey, a lonely touristic resort with a 12.5 miles long beach that competes with Varadero for the longest beach in Cuba. Its main attraction is its jade green waters, golden sand, and its coral reefs. It is always busy with divers. Center and below, t*he Parque Gonzalo de Quesada* or *Parque Casino Campestre,* at the other side of the bridge that crosses the Hatibonico River. It has a monument dedicated to the Spanish aviators Mariano Barberán and Joaquín Collar, who made the first non-stop flight between Sevilla and Camagüey before it tragically disappeared on its way to Mexico. Below, *Playa Bonita*, in Cayo Sabinal, a paradisiac beach where you can go for a ride in a catamaran in its crystalline waters.

Photos: On top, *the Gallo de Morón*. The municipality of Morón, founded in 1643, is known as the city of the rooster due to a verse about that animal, who went on singing after being plucked. It is in the north of Ciego de Ávila, surrounded by lush vegetation and wonderful beaches. At the entrance to the city is located its symbol, a bronze monument of the *Rooster of Morón*. Nearby are the remains of *La Trocha*, an area of 31 miles with small forts spread on it, created by Spain as a defensive line to stop the advance of General Máximo Gómez troops during the Independence War. Center and below, The *Cruz de Santa Cruz del Sur* and a Memorial to this devastated town. The category 5 Hurricane of Santa Cruz del Sur in 1932, was the most dangerous cyclone in the history of Cuba. The cross indicates the height that sea level reached on that occasion, the statue in the square, with a similar size, pays tribute to the victims.

Photos: On top and center, *Puerto Padre*, a city dating back into the 16th century. In the mid-19th century, it began its transformation into an industrial center with the construction of its first sugarcane mill. The town played a key role in Cuba's wars of independence, and today is something of a tourist center. Its founders were Creole landowners of Castilian ancestry, and Catalan merchants. It is said it was the first spot in which Columbus landed in Cuba, rather than Bariay bay, further east in the province of Holguín. At the center, Puerto Padre's *Avenida Libertad*. Below, *Jardines del Rey* in the Sabana-Camagüey archipelago, one of the most outstanding group of cayos of the Caribbean. Around 1513, Diego Velázquez named the archipelago after King Ferdinand the Catholic, competing with other southern Cuban cayos, already named Jardines de La Reina in honor of Queen Isabella the Catholic.

Oriente province has the largest mountainous regions of Cuba, and one of its largest coffee productions, which is a major contributor to the region's economy.

The city of Bayamo, is one of the largest cities in eastern Cuba, established by Spanish conquistador Diego Velázquez de Cuéllar in 1513. This province is in the eastern most side of Cuba and it is one of the most populous province. An important big city is Holguín. It's believed that Cristopher Columbus landed near that city in 1492, declaring it *"the most beautiful land human eyes have ever seen."* Las Tunas is probably the least visited city in the area, although efforts are succeding to start a variety of artistic installations in its center, which has given it the nickname of the *"City of Sculptures"* within Cuba. Santiago de Cuba, the capital of Oriente, in the south of the province, is one of the most populated and historic cities of Cuba, and it has a long record of battles fought during Cuba's war for independence.

As is true with most of Cuba's provinces, Oriente relies heavily on agriculture to support its economy, though there are also high quantities of material resources like nickel and iron in the region.

Oriente has a total population of 3,930,000 persons, with a total surface area of 41,100 square miles.

Photos: On top, the *Cathedral of Santiago de Cuba*, at *Céspedes Park*. Originally, Santiago had its first Cathedral-to-be in 1522. Over the years it was destroyed by earthquakes in 1678, 1766, 1852 and 1932. In 1882 it received the title of *Minor Basilica* from the Holy See and became a national monument of Cuba in 1958. On the left, a view of the entrance to *Santiago's Bay* from the *Castillo de San Pedro de la Roca del Morro*, about 6 miles southwest of the city centre. The fortress was declared a World Heritage Site by UNESCO in 1997, and it is cited as the best preserved and most complete example of Spanish-American military architecture. On the right, a view of the bay from *Cayo Smith*, located at its very center; it was owned by the DuPont family from 1870 to 1954. During the war of 1868, troops led by Maximo Gomez, Flor Crombet, and Enrique Collazo attacked the colony of *La Socapa*, and its 184 residents sought refuge in "*El Cayo*."

Photos On top, a view of the *Morro de Santiago de Cuba,* a defense against raiding pirates. It was finished in early 1600s, designed by Juan Battista Antonelli, a member of a Milanese family of military engineers, on behalf of the governor of the city, Pedro de la Roca de Borja. By 1775, the fear of attacks had diminished, and the fortress was converted into a prison. On the center and bottom, two views of *Cayo Smith* at the center of Santiago de Cuba Bay; the photos show the entrance side of the bay at *La Socapa.* This small town is today a nice and popular beach resort; in 1870, at dawn, Máximo Gómez attacked it as part of his military actions in the War of Independence of 1868. The garrison had about 50 men and could not resist the insurgent onslaught setting it up in flames.

Photos: On top, a view towards the sea from inside the walls of the *San Pedro de la Roca Castle*, the 17th century fortification protecting Santiago and its bastions and batteries. At the center, a typical quiet and secluded street of Santiago. Below, the magnificent *calle Padre Pico* in the *Tivoli* neighborhood of Santiago, where 18th century French-colonial mansions sit side by side with 16th century structures, while locals gather on its shady edges to gossip, play dominoes, and watch visitors panting while making their ascent. The street has had various names: *Loma de Boca Hueca, Cuesta de Amoedo, Loma de Piedra, Calle de los Leganitos,* and *Loma del Corvacho.* It was built in 1899 with funding from the mayor of the city, Emilio Bacardí y Moreau, who declined the honor of giving it his name, in favor of the former Dean of the Cathedral, Doctor Bernardo Antonio del Pico y Redín. (Father Pico).

Photos: On top, the *Plaza del Himno Nacional de Bayamo*, built around 1516; the Cuban national anthem, "*La Bayamesa,*" was sung there for the first time in 1868. The plaza dates from 1740 but its surroundings were devastated by fire in 1869; on the left, the *Church of San Salvador de Bayamo*, at one side of the *Plaza del Himno*; the church was erected around 1516 and has resisted many historical tragic events in the city, especially the 1869 fire. Below, the *main altar of the Church of San Salvador*, donated by the Holy Roman Emperor Charles V in 1546. The altar is "*screened,*" like theatre scenery, by Titian's painting of the *Transfiguration of Christ*, and is revealed only during the festivals of Christmas, Easter, and the Transfiguration.

Photos: On top, *Bayamo's Boulevard*, an avenue with a succession of small parks, some with old telephone poles converted into works of art, plus the most diverse gastronomic establishments, all leading to a beautiful park, with two imposing statues: one of *Perucho Figueredo*, the man who gave Cubans the Bayamesa Hymn, the other dedicated to the most sublime of Cubans, *Carlos Manuel de Céspedes*. Below, two photos: the entrance to the *Santa Ifigenia Cemetery* in Santiago de Cuba, and the *Mausoleum in Santa Ifigenia* that holds the remains of José Martí. This necropolis is the resting place of many notable Cubans: *José Martí, Carlos Manuel de Céspedes, Antonio Maceo, Facundo Bacardí* and his son *Emilio, Mariana Grajales* and *María Cabrales*, Maceo's mother and wife, *Tomás Estrada Palma*, the *Martyrs of the Virginius*, and many others.

Photos: On top, the *Sanctuary of Nuestra Señora de la Caridad del Cobre*, designated patroness of Cuba by Pope Benedict XV in 1916. The Sanctuary was built in 1926 and it sits in the village *El Cobre*, near Santiago de Cuba. The devotion to *La Caridad* became immensely popular when on 19 May 1801, a royal edict from king Charles IV of Spain decreed that Cuban slaves from the El Cobre copper mines were to be freed, in honor of the Blessed Mother. The bottom two photos show the main altar of the Sanctuary and the image of the Virgen itself. The statue measures about 16 inches tall; her feet rest on a brilliant moon, while angels spread their golden wings on a silver cloud.

Photos: On top, the *Yumurí River* in Baracoa, the easternmost area in Cuba. People refer to Baracoa as an island within an island, a remote place where the isolation is tangible, and the atmosphere... utopian. In 1511, the Spanish colonizers established Baracoa as Cuba's first city, and it has almost remained isolated ever since because this coastal gem is surrounded by an impenetrable fortress of mountains that keep the town hidden from the rest of the island. Also on top, the *Faro Vargas,* a XIX century Cabo Cruz lighthouse, with a height of 105 feet. Below, the coast around *Cabo Cruz*, on the eastern border of the Gulf of Guacanayabo. The prevailing microclimate in this coastal area is dry and arid, due to exposure to the nearby and very hot waters of the Caribbean, the opposite of the nearby mountain chains. Nearby, there are famous caves full of bats and native reptiles, among other interesting specimens of fauna.

Photos: Four images of areas in the center of the province of Oriente. On top left, a colossal view of the *Yunque de Baracoa.* On the top right, the Church of the town of *Contramaestre.* In the colonial period, from 1510 to 1550, the town was an *Encomienda Minera*, and an important center of Aboriginal settlements, the most significant named *Baire, Mayye, Maibío, Guaninao,* and *Guayacanes*, which are currently small neighborhoods. Their names evolved to Baire, Baire Abajo, and Cauto Baire. Below, the *Town of Cueto,* close to the villages of Alto Cedro, Barajagua, Birán, and Marcané. On the right, Mayarí, a city with origins dating back to 1757, when Spanish colonists established the first farms there. This entire area had numerous settlements before the independence of Cuba, as it was a good mining region. Geologically, its origin was marked by two natural processes: the tectonic emergence of mountains like those of the Sierra Maestra, and the erosion caused the Cauto River. During colonial periods, the area had a limited slave population and many independent peasants. During the independence struggles, the area teemed with figures like *Céspedes, Masó, Moncada, Figueredo*, and heroic places like *Bayamo, Jiguaní, Baire,* and *Dos Rios.*

Photos: Top to bottom: the *Pico Turquino*, the highest point in Cuba, a name derived from the *azul turquesa* hues of its mountain sides. The *Gran Piedra*, a large rock of volcanic origin, measuring 167 ft long, 82 ft high, and 98 ft wide, with an estimated weight of more than 63,000 tons. The *Salto del Guayabo* in Holguín, made by two waterfalls with 290 and 417 feet of vertical fall respectively, which join at the top and made an imposing fall, with access by a path located on the Eastern sidehill of the cascades. Finally, the *City of Gibara*, founded in 1817, also known as *La Villa Blanca* (The White Town); it enjoys a beautiful and breezy landscape, with excellent architectural designs and a well-planned layout of streets.

Photos: On top, the *Parque Calixto García* of Holguín, a stunning monumental square located in the center of the city, and the old *Banco Nuñez*, confiscated by the Communists in 1960; the building now houses the Banco de Crédito y Comercio (BANDEC). Below: An aerial view of *Manzanillo*, a port city founded in 1784 on the Gulf of *Guacanayabo*, near the delta of the *Cauto River*; it has limited access by sea due to the coral reefs of *Cayo Perla*. Finally, the *twists and turns of the Cauto River*, the longest river in Cuba, and in the entire Caribbean, with a length of 230 miles.

Photos: On top, a night view of *Baracoa*, the easternmost city in Cuba, a Cuban jewel, hidden among mountain ranges with abundant and beautiful endemic vegetation, crystalline rivers and paradisiacal beaches, a unique exotic place in the whole island of Cuba. Center, the *Parque Peralta* in Holguín; in 1868 several government buildings were located in this area and, along with the rest of the city, they were besieged by Major General *Julio Grave de Peralta*. Once the city was taken, the flag of Carlos Manuel de Céspedes was raised on the Parish tower. Below, an aerial view of the bay of Santiago de Cuba. It was there that the famous and decisive naval battle of *Santiago Bay* took place on July 3, 1898, which resulted in a dreadful loss of the Spanish fleet led by *Pascual Cervera y Topete*.

Photos: On top, *Baracoa*, known as the First City, the oldest colonial city on the island. All its charm is located at the eastern end of the island, in the province of Oriente. It is, without a doubt, a unique exotic place in the whole island, as evidenced by the highly preserved treasure *Parque Nacional Alejandro de Humboldt*. In 1511, Diego Velázquez, seeing the beauty of Baracoa, decided that it had to become their first town founded in Cuba, and it was, under the name of "*Our Lady of the Assumption of Baracoa*." The wealth of these lands subjected Baracoa to constant confrontation between the native inhabitants and the Spanish for centuries, giving rise to interesting legends such as the one that relates the death of Chief Hatuey, who would rather burn in hell if Spaniards had access to paradise. Center, *Punta del Quemado Maisi*, the easternmost point of the island of Cuba, a gradual bend in the coastline, not recognizable by any prominent point such as a rock or lighthouse. Below, another view of the *Salto del Guayabo River* in Mayarí, the highest waterfall in Cuba, the main attraction of the *Mensura National Park*, nested within the Pinares de Mayari plateau, about 2 hours from the beach resort of Guardalavaca.

Photos: On top, *Parque José Martí at Songo La Maya*, a municipality in Oriente, located north-east of Santiago de Cuba, centered on the towns of La Maya and Alto Songo. This remote place became famous after a *Son Montuno* that relates when firefighters had to come down all the way from the heights of Songo to extinguish a fire in La Maya that had been set to cash on insurance. Center, *Puerto Boniato*, just eight kilometers from the historic center of the city of Santiago de Cuba, has one of the most spectacular views of the city, but is a challenge for any hiker who is not afraid of joint pain. The unique site in the mountainous geography of Santiago, as well as the highway that gives access to it, was built under the initiative of the military governor general of the island, Leonardo Wood in 1901. Below, *Banes*, a city near Holguín. It was a key area for the native Taino people before the arrival of the Spanish. Banes is close to Guardalavaca; a museum featuring the Taino culture is situated halfway between both towns. The name comes from the Taino word *Bani*, meaning "valley."

Photos: On top, a view of *Sierra Maestra* from the Ensenada de Mora in the southern coast of Oriente. It extends eastward from Cape Cruz, at the southern shore of the Gulf of Guacanayabo, to the Guantánamo River valley. The heavily wooded mountains rise sharply from the Caribbean coast, culminating in the *Pico Turquino*, Cuba's highest elevation, 6,476 feet above sea level. Center, a view of *Santiago de Cuba* from the east. It was founded by Diego Velázquez in 1514, and grew greatly and fast thanks to its large harbor and the nearby copper mines at El Cobre. It was the Cuban capital until 1553, when the capital was moved to Havana. Below, the *Sierra Cristal National Park*, extending over two municipalities, Mayarí and Sagua de Tánamo. The area is a territory of contrasts and natural beauties, with beautiful valleys, high mountains; elevated temperatures in the plains and very cool in the mountains, beaches of fine sand, extensive wetlands, and pine forests areas with great deposits of iron, nickel, cobalt, chromium and even gold.

SOME OLD PHOTOS FROM CUBA

Photos: top row: **Martí Street**, and **Martí Park** in Pinar del Rio (1918); Second row: **National Capitol** in Havana under construction (1926); Third row: **Construction of the Malecón** in Havana (1848); **Manzana de Gómez** (1917); Fourth row: **Streetcars of Havana** (1948), and **Steps to the University** of Havana under construction (1928).

Photos: top row: **Parque de la Libertad** and **Playa de Bellamar**, Matanzas (1928); Second row: hotel **San Carlos** and **Sanatorio de la Colonia Española** in Cienfuegos (1918); Third row: **Parque Agramonte** in Camagüey (1912), and **Parque Tarafa** in Nuevitas (1926); Fourth row: Corner of Saco and General García streets in **Bayamo** (1935), and **Arco de la Independencia**, Santo Tomás Street between San Pedro and Aguilera, in front of the **Diego Velázquez Home** in Santiago de Cuba (1902).

Photos: Top to Bottom, Left to Right. **Monument to the Maine**,1928. **Colegio de Belén**,1925. The demolished **Reparto Mercedes** for its dangerous proximity to the runway at Rancho Boyeros Airport, 1930. The **"lanchas," going from Havana to Regla**, across the bay, 1956. The removal of the **statue of Isabel II** from Central Park, 1903. A **funeral procession in Havana**, 1890. A sign at a **food market in Matanzas** in 1892. The **Rancho Boyeros Airport** in 1938.

Photos: Top to Bottom, Left to Right: **Inauguration of Estrada Palma**, May 20, 1902. **American Embassy** under construction, 1955. **Celebrations** on May 20 May 1902. **Cuban Presidential Palace** under construction. **Havana Carnival**, 1937. **Cuban Teachers at Harvard**, 1901. **Parque Maceo**, Havana, 1941. **Woolworth** (Ten Cent) Havana, 1949.

MEMORIES

Photos: Top to Bottom, Left to Right: **Neptuno Street** in 1900. **Guanajay**, 1932. **Omnibus Santiago-Habana** in 1921. The **Palacio de Bellas Artes** under Construction, 1948. **Plaza Cívica** en construcción, 1951. **Reina Street** in Havana, 1948; at the end, the *Iglesia de Reina*.

SOME OLD POSTAGE STAMPS FROM CUBA

MEMORIES 91

SOME PHOTOS OF CUBA UNDER MARXIST RULE

Cuba descended into chaos when it was taken over by Marxists. Hundreds of civilian and police officers were shot without legal trials, thousands of Cubans went into exile rather than live under Communism, hundreds of priests were deported, the Marxists invented a new currency and made, both rich and poor, impoverished and destitute.

MEMORIES 94

Within less than a year of destroying democracy in Cuba, the Communists confiscated all personal and business properties, both owned by Cubans and by foreigners. All political parties were dissolved and outlawed, making the Communists the only legal political party. The country fell into ruins, as shown in numerous buildings across Cuba deteriorating, and rubble and debris everywhere.

MEMORIES

Havana, and many other cities in Marxist Cuba, have hundreds of buildings that have suffered the neglect of the authorities, while the members of the *Nomenclatura* enjoy travels, multiple houses, vacation homes and investments in foreign lands. Any attempts to protest by common citizens are quickly and violently suffocated by the uniformed police or the covert *Brigades of Quick Response*.

Communism has turned Cuba into a derelict nation, and Cubans have been trying to escape from the island since 1959. For half a century there have been many recurrent protests that the government suffocates with violence, years of incarceration and death. Cuba does not cease to intervene in other countries at the expense of the lives of recruits for these foreign adventures. Drug cartels have found Marxists to be active investors and participants in the trade, and when discovered, the *caporegimes* are sent to firing squads. Youngsters are indoctrinated at school in all levels. It seems to have no end.

SOME MISTERY PHOTOS FROM CUBA
(Try to guess where they are. They are identified on the next page of this book)

1

2

3

4

MEMORIES 98

Keys to the mystery photos from Cuba:

1-**Fusterlandia**: Extensive public-art installations by 73-year-old local artist José Fuster, with colorful, whimsical mosaics, situated in the beach town of *Jaimanitas*, La Habana.
 See https://www.youtube.com/watch?v=D4eQoS7yHGY

2-**Female land crabs** migrating from their forest home to the coastline in order to release their eggs into the Caribbean Sea. This view is from an important highway in Sancti Spíritus.
 See https://www.youtube.com/watch?v=FcvdZasEIY0

3-**Concrete staircase** to nowhere, built to allow access to a swimming pool located just above the sea, but the project was abandoned; it had been intended to be located on the coast in Santiago de Cuba.

4-Black doll in the **Casa Templo de Santeria Yemaya**, a religion originated in West Africa, established for almost a century in Trinidad, Cuba.

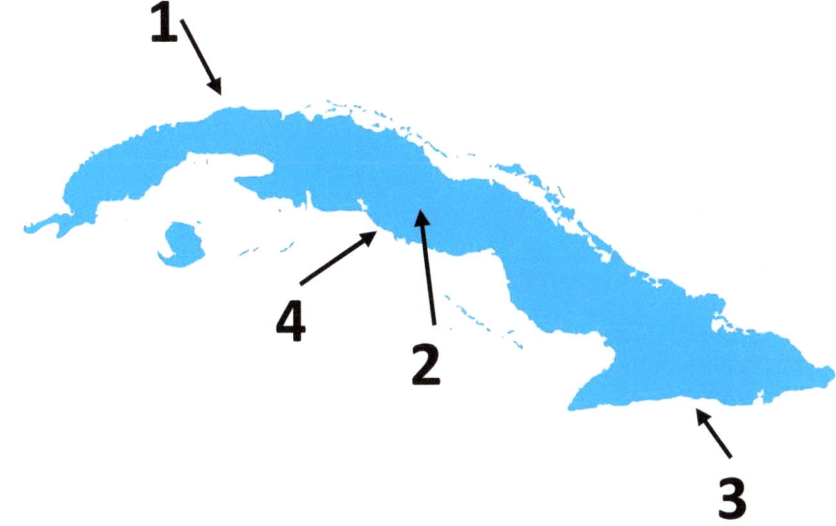

On top, two images created in the years where Cuba became Independent, early on the XX century. Below, Mariposa (*Hedychium coronarium*), Cuba's National Flower, and the Tocororo (*Priotelus temnurus*), Cuba's National bird, both endemic to the island of Cuba.

Raúl Eduardo Chao received his PhD from Johns Hopkins University and after a brief stint in industry spent 18 years in academe, as Full Professor and Department Chairman at the Universities of Puerto Rico and Detroit. In 1986 he founded a very successful management consultancy, assisting companies and government agencies to develop positive work environments and process improvement techniques as the means to secure simultaneous improvements in productivity and quality. The  Systema Group had as clients many Fortune 100 companies and Federal and State organizations, both in the US and abroad. Over the last thirty years, Chao has written forty three books and numerous articles in newspapers and reviewed journals. He and his wife Olga live in Lakeland, Florida.

www.ingramcontent.com/pod-product-compliance
Lightning Source LLC
Chambersburg PA
CBHW042017090426
42811CB00015B/1663